I AM:

A 40-DAY DEVOTIONAL

LAURIE McCARTY

WESTBOW
PRESS®
A DIVISION OF THOMAS NELSON
& ZONDERVAN

WestBow Press books may be ordered through booksellers or by contacting:

WestBow Press
A Division of Thomas Nelson & Zondervan
1663 Liberty Drive
Bloomington, IN 47403
www.westbowpress.com
1 (866) 928-1240

Because of the dynamic nature of the Internet, any web addresses or links contained in this book may have changed since publication and may no longer be valid. The views expressed in this work are solely those of the author and do not necessarily reflect the views of the publisher, and the publisher hereby disclaims any responsibility for them.

Any people depicted in stock imagery provided by Getty Images are models, and such images are being used for illustrative purposes only. Certain stock imagery © Getty Images.

Scripture marked (NKJV) taken from the New King James Version®. Copyright © 1982 by Thomas Nelson. Used by permission. All rights reserved.

Scripture quotations taken from the New American Standard Bible® (NASB), Copyright © 1960, 1962, 1963, 1968, 1971, 1972, 1973, 1975, 1977, 1995 by The Lockman Foundation Used by permission. www.Lockman.org

Scripture quotations marked (AMPCE) are taken from the Amplified Bible, Copyright © 1954, 1958, 1962, 1964, 1965, 1987 by The Lockman Foundation. Used by permission.

Scripture quotations marked (NIV) are taken from the Holy Bible, New International Version®, NIV®. Copyright © 1973, 1978, 1984, 2011 by Biblica, Inc.™ Used by permission of Zondervan. All rights reserved worldwide. www.zondervan.com The "NIV" and "New International Version" are trademarks registered in the United States Patent and Trademark Office by Biblica, Inc.™

ISBN: 978-1-9736-9303-1 (sc)
ISBN: 978-1-9736-9302-4 (e)

Library of Congress Control Number: 2020910112

Print information available on the last page.

WestBow Press rev. date: 07/07/2020

Contents

Preface

<u>I AM: A 40 Day Devotional</u> is an interactive, God-breathed tool to help you grow in your love and relationship with Jesus. Love opens healthy communication in our relationships. Our relationship with Jesus is no different. Each day includes a love letter to Jesus, a response, related Scripture, and a place to write your own love letter and Jesus's response to you. Prompt questions are also provided to help you as you journal.

God Himself inspired this devotional by answering I AM on a regular basis in His return letters. Many of the statements correspond to I AM statements in the Word. The first I AM statement in the Word is in Exodus 3:14 (NKJV) when God told Moses, "I AM WHO I AM" in response to Moses' question about God's name. Moses gave us a good picture of being one who spoke with God frequently as he sought relationship, wisdom, and strength. God met Moses every time and filled him with all he would ever need as he led God's people.

We too can have a respectful, awe-inspiring relationship with the King of kings and Lord of lords. Healthy relationships need healthy communication. Prayer is healthy communication with God. Many of us, however, have been trained how to speak prayers but not how to listen for the response. God can speak to us in so many ways and hearing His voice in our hearts is one of them.

If Jesus is your Lord and Savior, you will hear His voice on the inside of you! John 10:1-5 (NKJV) says,

"Most assuredly, I say to you, he who does not enter the sheepfold by the door, but climbs up some other way, the same is a thief and a robber. But he who enters by the door is the shepherd of the sheep. To him the doorkeeper opens, and the sheep hear his voice; and he calls his own sheep by name and leads them out. And when he brings out his own sheep, he goes before them; and the sheep follow him, for they know his voice. Yet they will by no means follow a stranger, but will flee from him, for they do not know the voice of strangers."

It is, therefore, imperative that you pray that God Himself would speak to your heart before you write. You will recognize the wise, loving, voice of God. Ask Him to help you discern the difference between His voice and your own thoughts. He will. He is good. When you hear the first words, begin to write.

His answers to you will always be loving and complete in grace and truth. They will agree with the Word. They will line up with God's character as we know it from the Word. They will ring true in your heart. The words are often profound and are sometimes words you have not thought of before. He will at times speak words of correction and redirection housed in love, grace, and mercy. Be encouraged by this, as Hebrews 12:6 (NKJV) says that the Lord disciplines the one He loves and chastens everyone He accepts.

Join me on a 40-day journey of vulnerability, love, faith, grace, and mercy. Draw close to the great I AM and grow in who *you* are, grow in your relationship with God, and grow in your Christ-likeness. May you be blessed as you journey through these 40 days of exploration and revelation!

Abbreviations

You will find Scripture references throughout this devotional. The abbreviations for the Bible versions used are:

AMPC – Amplified Classic Version
NASB – New American Standard Bible
KJV – King James Version
NKJV – New King James Version
NIV – New International Version

1

Dear Jesus,

Thank You for drawing me close. Your Spirit is giving me victory in many areas. You have set me free when I have allowed myself to be bound. I'm so glad Your Holy Spirit teaches me what Your Word means. Thank You for teaching me how to come near to You and how to find freedom and peace.

Forgive me for choosing weaker things—things that waste my time and energy. I'm so glad You lead me into the strong things, the things of Your Word, Your Spirit, and Your ways.

Everything You are is good. You are gracious and kind. Your love heals what ails me. When I embrace the fact that You love me without reservation, my whole mindset changes for the better. When I fully realize that fact, my heart heals. It makes me want to spend more time with You. Your presence makes me whole, and for that, I can never thank you enough. Hear my grateful heart today.

I'm excited about who You are. I'm eager to learn more. I ask You to lead me in all my ways.

Love,
Laurie

Dear Laurie,

My desire is that you become more like Me. When you become like Me, you become more gracious, kind, and bold. You become whole. I embody wholeness in every possible way.

Many resist Me, thinking they're protecting their freedom. If only they knew that running *to* Me and giving Me everything in exchange for *Me*—would give them true freedom and true joy. In doing so, they would become whole. If only they would perceive that I AM the King of the kingdom, the pearl of great price.

The wealth I have for you in the Spirit cannot be measured by human standards or by worldly means. Don't try to measure or compare.

Chase after Me with all your heart, and you will find Me. In so doing, you will find your life.

Love,
Jesus

Psalm 5:2 NASB

Heed the sound of my cry for help, my King and my God, for to You I pray.

Matthew 13:45-46 AMPC

Again the kingdom of heaven is like a man who is a dealer in search of fine *and* precious pearls, who, on finding a single pearl of great price, went and sold all he had and bought it.

1 Timothy 6:13-16 NASB

I charge you in the presence of God, who gives life to all things, and of Christ Jesus, who testified the good confession before Pontius Pilate, that you keep the commandment without stain or reproach until the appearing of our Lord Jesus Christ, which He will bring about at the proper time—He who is the blessed and only Sovereign, the King of kings and Lord of lords, who alone possesses immortality and dwells in unapproachable light, whom no man has seen or can see. To Him *be* honor and eternal dominion! Amen.

▶ **How well do you know the King? What can you do to seek Him in a greater way?**

2

Dear Jesus,

I put my hope in You, Lord. No one else can satisfy my soul like You. No one else embodies peace like You. No one else gives life like You. No one else gives grace like You. To whom else could I turn to receive what I need? Again, I have decided to put my hope in You!

I acknowledge You as my Master and my King. You are sovereign over all Creation. Your plans are not always what I understand, but I know they are good. Help me understand You more concerning Your thoughts and Your ways. And for those things that are mysteries to me, help me remember and trust that You know what You're doing. Increase my faith, and help me rest in Your goodness.

Your presence changes situations. I often think You present situations and wait for me to come to You. Even if the situations don't change, or don't change quickly, Your presence changes *me*. Your love calms me down. Your Word anchors my thoughts. My perspective changes, and I see things Your way.

I bow to You and to Your sovereignty. I humble myself before You, God.

Love,
Laurie

Dear Laurie,

Beauty is in your "crown" because you have realized who I AM. I am not only your personal Lord and Savior, but I AM your Master and your King.

Lay your "crown" at My feet once again, and I will add to it. I will polish it, and I will remove any damage that has been done to it. "Casting your crown" allows me to make it—your character—more beautiful. Those who refuse to "cast their crowns" at My feet are left with a dirty, damaged "crown" that is soiled by the flesh and the world.

A beautiful "crown" is one of submission and relationship. I AM the Creator of your "crown" (your character and all that is good in you). I continue to craft your "crown" as I lead you through life. Every weakness and fault that is laid at My feet can get cleaned and changed into something beautiful.

Those who cast a "crown" at My feet will have a clearer mind. Their thinking improves as I impart knowledge and wisdom into them. They enjoy better mental and emotional health. Their displayed faith is a shield to them. Their humility earns them favor they cannot gain anywhere else.

Enjoy receiving your "crown" from Me, and enjoy casting it at My feet. I must admit, one reason I enjoy having you cast your "crown" is that you must come near and visit Me to do so. Remember, I AM love.

Love,
Jesus

(Here, God uses the imagery of a crown to describe character; it is not meant to replace the truth of the Word that tells us we inherit an eternal, imperishable crown from Him.)

1 John 4:8 NKJV

He who does not love does not know God, for God is love.

1 John 4:16 NASB

We have come to know and have believed the love which God has for us. God is love, and the one who abides in love abides in God, and God abides in him.

▶ **In what ways will you allow God to love you every day? How can you increase your love for others?**

3

Dear Jesus,

Thank You for showing us how humility, patience, and meekness can be embodied in this life. You continually show us in Your Word how you served people, how You spoke to people, how You forgave people, and how You gave Your life for each one of us. Your authority and power are exalted in Your humility. Thank You for being willing to be all that and more for us. Your example is the one example we can follow to always get it right.

I often do not get it right. I know You're teaching me and training me. I'm so glad that every day is a new day in You. I want You to correct me! Correction doesn't always feel good, but when You correct me, it is done with grace, truth, and love. Even in that, You are the best example of how to live.

Forgive me for those moments when I neglect the right way. Remove from me pride, arrogance, and self-sufficiency. Draw me closer to You with Your humble heart and Your loving ways.

I am grateful You have shown me how to live well. Help me be more like You.

Love,
Laurie

Dear Laurie,

n the kingdom of God, holiness is uncompromising. It has no shades or variations but is filled with grace and truth. I AM the plumb line. I AM the standard by which all things are measured. Hearts are measured by Me; actions, words, and intentions are measured by Me.

The heart of man is prideful and self-centered. I have come so that hearts can be filled with Me. I have come to make hearts more like Mine. I have come to gather those that are willing. I have come to save the lost.

Aggression doesn't embrace those who don't know Me. Meekness, patience, and humility open the door to love. Love covers a multitude of sins. Love rights wrongs. Love heals the broken hearted. Love wins the battle. Love wins the race. Love is sovereign. I AM.

Love,
Jesus

Zechariah 4:9-10 NASB

"The hands of Zerubbabel have laid the foundation of this house, and his hands will finish *it*. Then you will know that the Lᴏʀᴅ of hosts has sent me to you. For who has despised the day of small things? But these seven will be glad when they see the plumb line in the hand of Zerubbabel—*these are* the eyes of the Lᴏʀᴅ which range to and fro throughout the earth."

▶ **Ask the Lord to be your standard or your plumb line so you can be in perfect alignment with Him. What changes will that mean for you?**

4

I AM YOUR TEACHER AND YOUR LORD

Dear Jesus,

I am grateful for You. You are always available to hear me. You help me when I don't even realize You are working on my behalf. You hold all things together, and You work things out. You resolve things that don't seem as if they could ever be resolved. You provide my hedge of protection and have protected me from things of which I am aware and likely also unaware. Your care for me is complete and amazing. Forgive me for ever taking all that for granted.

Thank You for doing a work in Your people. You help us, and as we work together, You help us more. You truly help us to love You and to love each other. Lord, help us love each other more! Show me how to get out of my own way and to let You work. I want transformation in my life so You will shine brighter in me. Help me focus so I can run after the things of Your heart and Your kingdom.

I open my eyes and my ears so I can follow You as You lead the way!

Love,
Laurie

Dear Laurie,

You may chase after Me as much as you want. I'll even let you catch up to Me. I relish the time talking with you. Come, rest on Me, and hand me your life's cares. You have allowed these cares to burden you. Burdened people don't hear Me as well, and I want you to hear My heart.

Ask Me to supply your needs for your own heart and for the ministries of grace and peace. I will hear you and will answer from heaven. I will send you all you need. The supply for your needs is limitless in Me. Don't let your mind limit what you ask Me. It pleases Me when you pray in faith and in trust.

Trust that I AM your Teacher and Your Lord. I call you a friend. I am here to teach you, to govern you, and to share with you. I will show you the way freely, generously, and lovingly. I do what is in your best interest. Continue to listen to Me and I will lead you.

Love,
Jesus

John 13:13 NASB

You call Me Teacher and Lord; and you are right, for *so* I am.

John 15:15 NASB

No longer do I call you slaves, for the slave does not know what his master is doing; but I have called you friends, for all things that I have heard from My Father I have made known to you.

▶ **What is Jesus teaching you today? How can you better realize His lordship and friendship in your life?**

5

I AM THE ROCK OF YOUR SALVATION

Dear Jesus,

I am grateful that Your nature is joyful. You knew Your purpose and Your path on earth. You knew that there would be great pain in Your sacrifice. All the while, You did not allow anything to steal Your joy. You showed us how to embody and to display joy. You showed us how to be both joyful and strong in truly dire circumstances. I am thankful that You show me how to be joyful and strong in my trying times.

Thank You for letting me near You and for letting me rest on You—that You would let me sit near You to learn and to listen. I find my heart comforted and lifted in Your presence. My heart rests in You. You steady me and focus me every day.

Lord, heal my heart with Your truth. Melt the hardness, the walls, and the shields. You know my life and the all the difficulties I have experienced. I know those experiences were never meant to harm me but to change me into a better person. Transform me into the person You planned for me to be.

Wash over me with Your voice. I need more joy and more strength. Help me, Lord.

Love,
Laurie

Dear Laurie,

I have always wanted you to be joyful. Joy is a fruit of the Holy Spirit. You are wise to come to Me to find your joy and your strength. I will indeed continue to help you.

Empty things and empty activities bring empty results, empty feelings, and an empty life. As Solomon wrote, "All is vanity." As you grow in Me, you will find things that once seemed life-giving are merely wasting your time. Their end is foolishness, and you will find that your precious time has dissipated.

Continue to seek those things that are solid. Continue to read My Word and find strength in the truth. My Word is solid, and My Word is truth. You will always find the answer and the way if you do so.

Chase after Me! I bring fullness and steadiness to you. I make up for what you lack. You will continue to find your time with Me fruitful, refreshing, and powerful. I know exactly what you need. I AM solid ground under your feet; I declare to you that I AM the Rock of Your salvation. Plant your feet on the truth of My Word. Let the truth of My saving grace fill you and transform you.

Love,
Jesus

1 Samuel 2:2 AMPC

There is none holy like the Lord, there is none besides You; there is no Rock like our God.

Psalm 95:1 AMPC

O come, let us sing to the Lord; let us make a joyful noise to the Rock of our salvation!

Ecclesiastes 1:14 NKJV

I have seen all the works that are done under the sun; and indeed, all *is* vanity and grasping for the wind.

▶ **What may you need to change in your life to make Him your true foundation?**

6

Dear Jesus,

I am eager to be in Your presence. There is so much in me that needs changing. In contrast to Your glory and perfection, I am not worthy to be in Your presence. I often feel "wrecked" as I enter Your presence and perceive Your holiness. Yet I realize Your sacrifice was for me, and I receive it. I apply Your gift of righteousness to my life. I am grateful for Your mercy.

I come to You again to receive grace. I need Your strength to do all You have asked me to do. I want to do things Your way and not be independent of You. I don't want to be critical or double-minded. I don't want to waver in my faith. I don't want to experience highs and lows in my emotions. I want the steadiness that comes with being connected to You.

I want to be where You are. I want to do Your will; teach me. I'm pressing in, knowing You are faithful.

Love,
Laurie

Dear Laurie,

I AM the Door. Only through Me and My saving grace can you enter the kingdom of God. You have chosen well to seek Me as such.

Thank you for taking the opportunity to defend Me, My Word, and My kindness. Most people have been led to believe that I am critical and harsh. They have been led to believe I am waiting for them to make mistakes and to punish them. I love them more than they understand. You have done much to teach and to encourage them with that fact. I want increasing righteousness in them, and I will help them get there. I want greater relationship with each person. I love each one, and I am eager to lead them into My kingdom.

I know your work inside the four walls of the church is what you are now used to. Please remember the church is not a building. You are the church, and the kingdom of God is wherever you go. Your work outside the four walls of the church will not be difficult. I will set up divine appointments for you.

Take time in your life to *be*: Be peaceful. Be righteous. Be faithful. Be joyful.

Let My fruit grow in you. Pay attention to Me in this, and I will teach you how to *be.* Not everything in life was meant to be *doing* and rushing. Give yourself permission to *be* in this manner. It will indeed strengthen you, and it will bring you further in the transformation you seek.

Knock on the Door and come in.

Love,
Jesus

John 10:6-9 AMPC

Jesus used this parable (illustration) with them, but they did not understand what He was talking about. So Jesus said again, I assure you, most solemnly I tell you, that I Myself am the Door for the sheep. All others who came [as such] before Me are thieves and robbers, but the [true] sheep did not listen to *and* obey them. I am the Door; anyone who enters in through Me will be saved (will live). He will come in and he will go out [freely] and will find pasture.

▶ **How can you truly be reminded that Jesus is your Door to salvation?**

7

I AM YOUR KEEPER

Dear Jesus,

Thank You for hearing my prayers and for leading the way with Yourself —Your Word. I pray Your Word rises up in me with power. Sort out the things of my own flesh from the things of Your Spirit. Lord, I ask You to do a mighty work in me.

You are glorious, kind, and wonderful. You're the reason I'm here. Thank You for making me more able than I am. Thank You for feeding me wisdom that I don't naturally have. Help me to be more in line with You and with Your thoughts. Help me to be more motivated and focused than I am. Help me to be more peaceful and trusting than I am. With You, I can.

Your Word is true. You are faithful, loving, and long-suffering. All thanks and glory to You.

Love,
Laurie

Dear Laurie,

If all glory goes to Me, why do you seek glory from man? I will heal you from every insecurity, from every offense, and from every pain—if you let Me. Give it all to Me, and I will heal you. Truly, I will heal every wound.

Pride must continue to come away from you. Be ever so careful. Pride is insidious and evil. It can sneak into your heart and into your thoughts in subtle ways. Ask the Spirit to help you hold every thought captive to My obedience. Allow Me to help you filter your thoughts for your own good. It is good for you to see through My eyes and to hear through My heart.

My Name is holy. Thank you for honoring My Name in all situations. As you honor Me and My Name, I receive honor, and the hearts of people are changed.

Do not be afraid. I AM your keeper. I will keep you from true harm. I will keep you for your sake, for the sake of the kingdom, and for fellowship with Me forever.

Love,
Jesus

Psalm 121:5 NASB
The LORD is your keeper;
the LORD is your shade on your right hand.

Isaiah 42:6 NKJV
I, the LORD, have called You in righteousness,
And will hold Your hand;
I will keep You and give You as a covenant to the people,
as a light to the Gentiles,
to open blind eyes,
to bring out prisoners from the prison,
those who sit in darkness from the prison house.

▶ **In what ways does God demonstrate Himself as your keeper? How can you be reminded of these today?**

8

Dear Jesus,

My heart and mind are troubled when things seem out of order in me, in my surroundings, and in the world. I thank You that You are trustworthy, and that You will defend what is right. I ask that You work everything out for the very best outcome. Let Your Name be honored and Your ways be known and displayed. Heal the hurting, and avenge the blameless. Grant wisdom to all of us, and let peace rule and reign. Bring peace to my heart as I lay these petitions before You.

Why is it that when one or two things are not right in my life, I descend in my thinking? Why do I forget all the things that are going right? Lord, have mercy! Heal my body, and heal my mind! I need Your healing touch!

In all reality, I am blessed. You have put me in a pleasant place in so many areas of my life. Your grace and Your favor are evident. Your presence is like a vessel that is filled to overflowing with good things. You are worthy of praise and adoration.

Love,
Laurie

Dear Laurie,

It is your adoration I seek. It is your devotion I seek. It is your heart I seek. Hold fast to the teachings I have given you. Remember the truths you have known since childhood.

Don't let your heart be troubled or distracted by the enemy's tricks. You have the ability to pass the test and to win the prize. Stand firm and watch Me work. I AM the one who heals. I AM the one who makes blessings out of curses. I AM the one who defends you. I will bring you through.

Enjoy the pasture I've given you in which to feed. It is a good place to be. Don't miss it! Listen to My leading and yes, even My whisper, at every move. I will supply all you need to accomplish what I have laid out for you. March forward with courage, and shine My light. You can do it. I AM with you every step of the way.

I want you to develop a greater culture of honor within yourself—how you see and help others. Help others develop their gifts and talents for Me and for the kingdom. Just as others have helped you learn and grow, help others learn and grow according to how I have made them and gifted them.

Observe each person and each situation with a pure heart and clean eyes. Listen to My still, small voice! I will open up ways and opportunities that will bring progress and excitement for each one and for the kingdom! Watch what I can do in them and in you!

Love,
Jesus

Exodus 15:26 NIV

He said, "If you listen carefully to the LORD your God and do what is right in his eyes, if you pay attention to his commands and keep all his decrees, I will not bring on you any of the diseases I brought on the Egyptians, for I am the LORD, who heals you."

Psalm 103:1-5 NKJV

Bless the LORD, O my soul;
and all that is within me, *bless* His holy name!
Bless the LORD, O my soul,
and forget not all His benefits:
Who forgives all your iniquities,
Who heals all your diseases,
Who redeems your life from destruction,
Who crowns you with lovingkindness and tender mercies,
Who satisfies your mouth with good *things,*
so that your youth is renewed like the eagle's.

▶ **What area of your life needs God's healing? Ask Him and let Him speak to you today.**

9

I AM THE MESSIAH

Dear Jesus,

Thank You for finishing the work for my freedom. I am amazed that Your sacrifice and Your blood are so complete; they will always be more than enough. Thank You for Your Spirit who leads me and teaches me how to live in that freedom and righteousness. Thank You for every bit of progress and for every victory.

Your love for me is more than I can realize and comprehend. My mind cannot fathom how deep and complete is that love. I want to grow in understanding of that love. Help me to know You more. I know my sitting and my listening will open up the door for further revelation.

God, show me another facet of Your character today! You could show me another facet every day for all eternity, and yet there would be more. I am continually amazed that You are infinite and wonderful.

Open my eyes to Your wonders. Help me see both the small and the great things You do. You have continued to show me Your amazing Creation in people, in nature, in seasons, and in life itself. Your wonders are often simple and profound as well as great and glorious. I am in awe of You.

Love,
Laurie

Dear Laurie,

Your name means laurel crown. I AM the One who crowns you with righteousness, with favor, and with loving-kindness. It is My right and My desire to do so.

Do not allow others to make you feel badly that your path differs from theirs. Let My light shine through you in the way *I* have ordained. Stand up with kind confidence, and help those who are weak and struggling. Help them to see Me more clearly.

Pull down strongholds wherever I show you to do so. Speak to the scales, and they will fall off the spiritual eyes. Cause the light to shine in places that need My light and revelation. Speak My Word with life, power, and authority. Declare My truth with faith and hope!

Trust Me in all things. I have the power to do great and mighty things. Open your heart to truly believe in Me. The Father has shown you that I AM the Messiah, the Son of the Living God. Know that My Father has sent Me, and I have done all that He sent Me to do. You have victory in Me.

Love,
Jesus

Matthew 16:15-17 NIV

"But what about you?" he asked. "Who do you say I am?" Simon Peter answered, "You are the Messiah, the Son of the living God." Jesus replied, "Blessed are you, Simon son of Jonah, for this was not revealed to you by flesh and blood, but by my Father in heaven."

John 4:25-26 NKJV

The woman said to Him, "I know that Messiah is coming" (who is called Christ). "When He comes, He will tell us all things." Jesus said to her, "I who speak to you am *He.*"

▶ **Do you fully believe that Jesus is the Messiah? Ask Him to help you grow in your understanding of Him as the wonderful, long-awaited Christ.**

10

Dear Jesus,

Thank You for helping me with all the tasks that needed to be completed, and for leading me through all that needed to be prayed. Thank You for the direction and the revelation by Your precious Holy Spirit. As always, thank You for hearing and for answering my prayers. May I never take that for granted.

My soul is rising up with joy and thanksgiving for all that You are. I give You honor as the King of kings and as the Lord of lords. I delight in who You are. I bless Your Name, Lord.

Lord, as Your church body, speak over us, sing over us, and thunder over us. We need Your relationship and Your righteousness. We want to live in the power of Your kingdom! May we have full fellowship with You and with each other. God, make a way for Your church!

Lord, reveal more of You to me and to us! We want to know You more. We want to see Your glory!

Love,
Laurie

Dear Laurie,

Answers are for the seekers. Treasures are for the finders. Open doors are for those who knock. Revelation is for the pure in heart.

Reverence yourself before the Giver of all light. Humble yourself before the King of all kings. Spend time in My glory. All of these will change you greatly. Your internal atmosphere will change.

Immerse yourself in the Holy Spirit before you read My Word. He will teach you, and He will show you things you have not yet seen. I wish for you to have increased knowledge in My Word. There are things only He can show you as you read and study. The natural man cannot see these things. You need Him to teach you more. In doing so, you will not be deceived, and you will not be dismayed by anything that happens.

The eve of this age is coming. Light needs to shine in a deep darkness. I AM the Light of the world. Cause Me to shine—through you and through all who will allow Me to shine in them. So, let your light shine.

Love,
Jesus

John 8:12 AMPC

Once more Jesus addressed the crowd. He said, I am the Light of the world. He who follows Me will not be walking in the dark, but will have the Light which is Life.

Matthew 5:8 NASB

Blessed are the pure in heart, for they shall see God.

Matthew 5:16 NASB

Let your light shine before men in such a way that they may see your good works, and glorify your Father who is in heaven.

▶ **How can you increase the light of Jesus in your life? How can you allow Him to shine through your life in a greater way?**

11

Dear Jesus,

Thank You for always being with me in good times and in bad times. Thank You for hearing my prayers and for refreshing my tired spirit. Thank You for walking with me through this season.

Your grace toward me and Your hedge of protection are so appreciated. Your wonderful grace is neither earned nor deserved, and I am aware of that. I owe You everything. Your presence is priceless, matchless, and all-powerful. I am forever grateful.

I pray that You continue to show Yourself strong in this challenging season. I know Your goal is that we would all love each other with Your love. You teach us through every situation and circumstance. You help us love one another when sometimes it seems impossible. Continue to heal my heart from the sins of judgment and offense. Heal my heart fully so I can trust You in all situations.

Speak to my heart today, Lord. Cause my heart to be flexible and obedient. Grant me the grace to be all You want me to be.

Love,
Laurie

Dear Laurie,

Time is of the essence. The more swiftly and completely you agree with My Word and obey it, the easier it will be for you. You are at a place where you could be living more completely in the fruit of the Spirit. You are growing, but sometimes you live in the fruit of your own mind. You want transformation? Here is a perfect opportunity to grow, to have victory, and to achieve the unity you desire. In all of it, you will find healing for your soul.

Rest yourself completely upon Me. Stop striving. Be still and know that I AM God. I will fight for you. There is no need to feel badly. There is no need to complain. Repent of your wrong thinking and of your wrong attitude. Hand it all over to Me and watch Me do a work in you! I am eager to help you. You want to get it right, and I encourage you to take this opportunity to do so.

Live in the joy of your salvation. Live in the peace that I AM. Live in the faith and sure knowledge that no one can derail My plan for you, except you. Live in the reality of My love that rules over all things and overwhelms all things.

Delve into My Word and My Spirit like never before. Avail yourself of every opportunity to read and to pray. Learn of Me and know My wise, forgiving nature. Again, I say, time is of the essence.

Love,
Jesus

Psalm 46:10 NIV
He says, "Be still, and know that I am God;
I will be exalted among the nations,
I will be exalted in the earth."

▶ **What is going on in your life right now that you could hand over to God? In what areas of your life can you trust Him more? Be still and know that He is God!**

12

Dear Jesus,

It's been a while since I've written. I'm so sorry, my beautiful Jesus. I cannot even reason why I would neglect the one who loves me the most. You show up with such grace, power, and purpose. I love it when You come to me with tools to help me in life. I love it when You encourage me and refresh me. You are always kind.

Thank You for the blessings of a Godly husband and loving children. Thank You for Your Holy Spirit—He is the best gift You could have ever given me! He is the best at guiding me back to where I need to be in every season of life.

Thank You for helping me experience improved health. I trust You to work out the administrative challenges that accompany health management. Help me to do my part, and I thank You that You do Your part. You show me favor. You truly are the God who heals. You are magnificent!

Love,
Laurie

Dear Laurie,

I t *has* been too long! I've heard you calling My Name. I've seen you fear in situations when I'm asking you to trust Me. I have you in the palm of My hand. Don't worry about the future and the decisions you will need to make. Listen to Me day by day, and I will lead you by My Spirit. I have your days written in My book. It is under control.

I'm doing something *in* you first. Your disciplined prayer and study will cause you to grow by leaps and bounds.

I'm the one who sees you. I'm the one who moves you to where you belong. I know the path I've put you on, and nothing surprises Me. I know where you are. I will bring you to the best place for *you.*

Rest in My presence and absorb Me. Strengthen yourself in Me. I AM the God who sees. Trust My eyes. Trust My heart. Trust My plan. I will never mislead you.

Join Me in the dance of your life. Do you remember at your lowest moment in life that I invited you to dance and rejoice in Me? I loved you without reservation then, and I love you without reservation now. I gave up My life up for you. My Father gave Me My life back and has given Me all authority. All you need is Me. Rest in Me. I see you, and I have you covered.

Love,
Jesus

Genesis 16:13 NASB
Then she called the name of the Lord who spoke to her, "You are a God who sees"; for she said, "Have I even remained alive here after seeing Him?"

Psalm 56:8 AMPC
You number *and* record my wanderings; put my tears into Your bottle—are they not in Your book?

▶ **What steps can you take to live in the confidence that He sees you and loves you?**

13

Dear Jesus,

Thank You for another new day. Your beauty fills me and surrounds me. Your holiness shines its beauty on all Your Creation.

Oh! Thank You for allowing me to see a momentary glimpse of the heavenly kingdom at work among Your gathered people! The beautiful angels at work—the one with the beautiful blue dress spreading Your glory, and the joyful, dancing angels keeping the beat of the worship. I was awed by the angelic conductor moving his whole self to worship, and to bring all the worship together in the church. You are amazingly creative—You created creativity! Thank You for sending and directing Your angels to help us glorify You.

Your presence was surely known as fruit came forth in the preaching and prayer. Many were drawn closer to You. You know just what we need and when we need it. Thank You for always being present. You change everything. I praise Your Name!

Love,
Laurie

Dear Laurie,

There was more going on than you saw. I sent multitudes to join you, to encourage you, to minister to you, and to protect you. I AM WHO I AM and I will not leave you without help as you go about My work.

The walls are coming down. There are many yet to remove, but the walls are indeed coming down. Walls between people are coming down. Each person has a place in My house and in My kingdom.

Holiness is part of My being. Holiness is My natural state—part of My divine nature. It is innate to Me, and I wish it to be innate to you. Allow My Spirit to swallow up and to conquer the flesh—the human nature in you. I AM WHO I AM dwells within you, overcoming all that would harm, all that would distract, all that would corrupt, and all that would kill.

Value My Spirit within you and do not grieve Him. His nature is holiness, truth and life. You could not have received a better gift. All else pales in comparison.

Be made whole. All that you need, I have in the palm of My hand—ready to give. I'm waiting for you to ask. Immerse yourself in Me, and receive.

Abundantly Yours,
Jesus

Exodus 3:13-14 NASB

Then Moses said to God, "Behold, I am going to the sons of Israel, and I will say to them, 'The God of your fathers has sent me to you.' Now they may say to me, 'What is His name?' What shall I say to them?" God said to Moses, "I AM WHO I AM"; and He said, "Thus you shall say to the sons of Israel, I AM has sent me to you.'"

▶ We serve the mighty I AM WHO I AM! How can you adjust your mind and heart to get excited about this truth?

14

Dear Jesus,

Thank You for taking such good care of me. You bless me as You feed, soothe, restore, and correct me. You always correct me in love. You cause righteousness to exist within me. You lead me in Your perfect balance of grace and truth.

The valley of the shadow of death is just that—a shadow. Because You are full of light, the shadow is a sign of Your presence in that valley. Even when I feel like darkness surrounds me, I know Your presence is with me. I take great comfort in knowing that You are near.

I just realized that the main job of the sheep is to eat, drink water, follow the shepherd, and rest. All the while, I thought that I needed to constantly strive to please You and others. I now realize that I've had it wrong. Lord, have mercy. Lead me to feed on Your Word, drink of Your Spirit, obey You, and rest in Your goodness.

May I dwell with You forever!

Love,
Laurie

Dear Laurie,

I AM your Good Shepherd. I have always been a place for you to find rest, restoration, and victory. My rod and My staff are truly a comfort as I correct you and guide you. They are beneficial and instrumental in the valley. How else would you get out of the valley? You cannot find your own way out. Many get stuck in the valley. Their own ways and their own thinking slow them down, and they cannot see in the shadows.

That is the place you were in. You could not see correctly, and you could not see the light in the midst of the shadows. I have come and caused righteousness to be stirred up in you and sight to be restored to you.

There is a beautiful place in My presence that has green pastures for you to feed on and to rest upon. My still waters are always available to you. I will lead you to rest beside the still waters. Come rest. Be restored in your body, soul, and spirit. Be rid of old things and old ways of seeing and thinking. Come out of the valley, and dine with Me at the table.

I will and do anoint your head with oil, and I have a seat for you at the table. Come out of the valley, and take your place in My presence. Guilt and shame are things of the past. Come, take your place.

Love,
Jesus

Psalm 23:1 NASB
The LORD is my shepherd,
I shall not want.

John 10:11, 14 NIV
I am the good shepherd. The good shepherd lays down his life for the sheep.
I am the good shepherd; I know my sheep and my sheep know me— just as the
Father knows me and I know the Father—and I lay down my life for the sheep.

▶ **How will you let your Good Shepherd lead you, correct you, and comfort you today?**

15

I AM GOD ALMIGHTY

(As part of the backstory here, my sister was given an unexpected stage 4 cancer diagnosis. We and our extended family were experiencing shock, disbelief, sadness, and a sense of foreboding that rattled us to our very core.)

Dear Jesus,

I am in shock right now. My thoughts are confused, and my knees feel weak. All this time, she didn't feel well. I wish I had paid better attention, and I wish there was more I could do. I pray for her, and I will keep on praying for her. Thank You for answered prayer. Thank You for giant waves of grace in the midst of this giant storm. I know You're in this storm with us, and it helps to know we're not alone.

I ask You to impart Your peace on the inside of me and on the outside. Calm my thinking so I can help her make good decisions. Help me be there for her. Help me be part of the support system in the spiritual and in the natural realms. As a minister, this is not new for me. As a family member, it's all new to me. I really don't know what to do.

God, You know that she and I know each other better than any other. You know close siblings are wonderful friends and have known each other the longest. She's always been there, and I don't dare to think what life would be like without her. I'm asking You for help.

God, in the midst of this trial, cause miracles to happen! May she know You like never before. Rescue her life, and give her strength! You are a God of miracles!

Hear my heartfelt prayers today and every day, God.

Love,
Laurie

Dear Laurie,

I encourage you to be there for her. Be present, and follow her lead in what she needs. In fact, be present in every relationship in your family. You are all feeling and experiencing this. There is no need to hide your emotions out of pride. There is no need to fear. Be yourself. Pay attention, and listen well. Let her know of your love for her. There will be moments when you will need to advocate for her. There will be other moments where her immediate family will need your presence as well. Listen well to My Spirit and obey.

Your next level of servanthood is arising. Your servant heart is being polished and refined. Your kindness is being rounded out. Your words are becoming smoother and more gracious. You are more aware to let Me filter every thought in your mind, every emotion in your heart, and every word that comes from your mouth.

My grace is on you and in you. You can do everything I'm asking of you. You can do everything I say you can do. You can do everything that's needed in the circumstance and in the moment.

Remember that I know everything and I AM alive forever. I AM God Almighty. Use My Name and all the authority I've given you. Pray, and trust in Me.

Love,
Jesus

Genesis 17:1 NASB

Now when Abram was ninety-nine years old, the LORD appeared to Abram and said to him,

"I am God Almighty; walk before Me, and be blameless."

Genesis 35:11-12 AMPC

And God said to him, I am God Almighty. Be fruitful and multiply; a nation and a company of nations shall come from you and kings shall be born of your stock; the land which I gave Abraham and Isaac I will give to you, and to your descendants after you I will give the land.

▶ **Look to the Lord today and ask Him to give you a greater sense of Him as God Almighty. How can that help you see difficulty, death, and grief differently?**

16

I AM THE WAY, THE TRUTH, AND THE LIFE

(This was written two days before my sister passed. God's strength was pivotal in her and in praying for her as she transitioned into everlasting glory with Jesus.)

Dear Jesus,

I continually speak out Your Name as a prayer. Thank You for carrying me through. Thank You for giving me the energy and resources to parent, to work, to bless, and to feed. I sense the water of Your Spirit running through the dry riverbed, surrounding each stone, and flowing around each obstacle. I know You're helping me every step of the way. I see You helping my sister.

Thank You for Your unending grace. I sense Your grace supporting me. Let Your grace flow in me and through me. May it continue to help me, and may it give You glory. May it advance the King and His kingdom. Arise, shine! Cause my heart to be lifted; cause my countenance to shine and to honor You.

Thank You for giving me some time alone with my sister as she transitions from this life to the next. I am so appreciative that You set up another divine appointment for us so I could pray for her with freedom, and I could see joy on her face as she sensed Your presence. Oh, a memory to last forever! I can never thank You enough for helping her! God, You are so good to us. Thank You for drawing her close to You. I bless Your Name.

Love,
Laurie

Dear Laurie,

Hold on to Me, for I AM the Way, the Truth, and the Life. I do have all things under control. I do have everything in the palm of My hand. Connect with Me continually, and I will show you things that will comfort your heart. Let My Word be a steadying force for you. Let My Spirit wash through you.

I will reconcile all things concerning this life. Time in My kingdom is not the same as the world's sense of time. You will see. Someday, you will see and understand what I am saying to you.

You have a partial, or fractured understanding of what is happening right now. I see it as a whole process in light of eternity and in light of My goodness. Please believe that, and form your thoughts and decisions based on these truths.

Rest in Me, as My grace is upon you. You cannot earn My grace. I simply give it to you.

Love,
Jesus

John 14:6 AMPC

Jesus said to him, I am the Way and the Truth and the Life; no one comes to the Father except by (through) Me.

▶ **How is Jesus the Way for your life and for eternity? Ask Him to show you today!**

17

Dearest Jesus,

Thank You for creating opportunities for me to speak to my sister about You and about eternity. When put in the dire life-and-death position, she knew she wanted to make a decision about her forever. She had read much about You and knew You, but not necessarily as her Savior. You heard her pray with all her heart. What a blessing for her to know that You heard her prayers!

The ensuing hours and days were very sad and stressful for all of us. Because of You, she waited for her time to leave this earth with more love in her heart than ever. You made her loving and sweet, and she became that all the more. Thank You for the blessing of a good sister.

Thank You for giving me courage to face the fear of loss. Only with You can fear be conquered. You are the victory inside of me. Thank You for giving me courage to speak a eulogy that honored her, her husband and son, and You.

Living every day without her here is going to be a challenge, and a sad one at that. I am asking now for help every day so I can process grief in a healthy way. I am asking that You will comfort my heart. To be honest, I'm not looking forward to this process and the "new normal" it presents. I ask again; Lord, help me.

Love,
Laurie

Dear Laurie,

I will keep proving My faithfulness to you so you will understand that I AM strong enough, wise enough, and present enough to help you with all you need. I AM all you need for victory within. I AM the Resurrection and the Life! I declare victory *in* you! You have experienced great loss before, but this one hit very close to home. Take comfort in the fact that she is with Me.

For you, don't let sadness or grief prevent you from entering My presence. Rejoice in Me! Give Me glory, and I will display My glory around you. I seek hearts who are pure before Me. Rest in My presence. Some would want you to believe that entering My presence is difficult, or requires hard work. It does not. Come and rest.

Allow yourself to grieve. If you're looking to Me as an example, remember that I cried when I grieved for Lazarus. It's okay to let your guard down and weep. Don't allow pride or self-sufficiency to kick in. You ask Me to help you. I most surely will. And I AM helping you, even right now.

Love,
Jesus

John 11:25-26 NASB

Jesus said to her, "I am the resurrection and the life; he who believes in Me will live even if he dies, and everyone who lives and believes in Me will never die. Do you believe this?"

▶ Because Jesus was resurrected from the dead, He has gone before us! He has paved the way of victory for you! How does this truth help you today?

18

Dear Jesus,

You are absolutely and completely magnificent in Your presence and in all Your ways. Your character is loving and perfect. Your knowledge of me is complete. You cause me to rest in my soul, because of Your complete goodness toward me.

Thank You for giving me constant reminders of Your goodness. You remind me that You have conquered death. You remind my heart of what You have done for my loved ones who are now with You. You remind me of what You have done for me. I rejoice in these truths.

Lord, I ask You to help the body of Christ minister to people as You see fit. Help us coordinate within and without the four walls of the church. Help us work together well. We want to see the fruit of our labor and the fruit of the labor of those before us. I am reminded that the church belongs to You, not us.

May Your presence be a place where we can feed, rest, and be all that You want us to be.

Love,
Laurie

Dear Laurie,

You are precious. You do not fail to give Me glory. Your understanding of who you are and who I AM serves the body of Christ. Thank you for reminding people that I AM the Head of the church! Thank you for listening to My Spirit and for helping My body.

I have more plans for you. You have been passing more and more tests. Keep praying and keep listening to My Spirit. Ask for help with your heart and with your self-control. Keep command of your heart and tongue, and you will gain more respect. You will bring more value to those who need you.

Delve into My Word more and more. I have so much for you to learn! There are fallacies and deceptions that need to be removed from the minds and hearts of My people. Study and learn. Listen to My voice in the midst.

Continue to enact the small things—the kind words, the niceties, the words of thanks, the notes, and the anonymous blessings. I see all that you do in secret.

Enjoy your life. I have restored you, and I have given you abundance.

Love,
Jesus

Ephesians 1:22-23 AMPC

And He has put all things under His feet and has appointed Him the universal and supreme Head of the church [a headship exercised throughout the church], Which is His body, the fullness of Him Who fills all in all [for in that body lives the full measure of Him Who makes everything complete, and Who fills everything everywhere with Himself].

▶ **How can you better find your place in the body of Christ? How can you give Jesus, the Head of the church, greater glory?**

19

Dear Jesus,

Your grace and Your power continue to carry me. Obviously, You are aware of life's difficulties that have happened these last few months. You did say You would work it all out and take care of it. I'm trusting You to continue to carry me through into wholeness.

Thank You for Your presence today, and for showing Yourself strong for Your people. I pray all our eyes are opened to Your immensity, infinity, and complete power. Thank You for leading me in prayer and ministry for Your faithful ones. I truly love them.

Lord, continue to show me how to *be.* Continue to stir up Your Spirit in me to settle my spirit and soul. Send Your Word and heal me. Thank You for continuously reminding me of the power of Your Word. Lord, teach me. Continue to teach me how to rest at Your feet, how to sit by You and listen, and how to be immersed in Your Spirit.

Blessed be Your Name,
Laurie

Dear Laurie,

I watch you struggle and try to do everything without full rest. You have been trying to do things in your own strength. You have been grieving and sad, and you have held on to those emotions. You try to juggle everything well in life. You try to keep all the balls in the air and not let any drop. What you don't fully realize is that juggling is a skill; it is a game where you eventually have to stop. Your body, your eyes, and your brain get tired. You have limits. I don't. That's why it's wise to give things to Me, and to let Me lead. I know the way. I AM the Lord of the Sabbath. Learn of Me.

I have a good season in store for you. One of healing and growth. Some things *in* you will be shaken and healed! You have some old mindsets, fears, and hurts that have to go. They're holding you back, and they're hurting you. Don't be afraid of the process. I will see you through to the best result.

Cover yourself and your family in prayer. They need the prayer. Ask Me, and I will defend them.

Love,
Jesus

Matthew 12:7-8 AMPC

And if you had only known what this saying means, I desire mercy [readiness to help, to spare, to forgive] rather than sacrifice *and* sacrificial victims, you would not have condemned the guiltless. For the Son of Man is Lord [even] of the Sabbath.

▶ **What area of your life needs God's rest? What will you do to let Jesus be your Lord of the Sabbath?**

20

Dear Jesus,

I am so grateful that You came to show us the Father's nature. I am grateful that You live forever. I am grateful for Your complete authority. All we are, all we have, and all we do belong to You.

You are the reason for my faith. Thank You for giving me this precious faith on which to cling. Thank You that faith is not static but can be used, grown, multiplied, and given away.

You do good in us and amongst us. I tend to look around me and see things that aren't right. I've come to realize that You want me to work on things within *me* that aren't lined up with You. Oh, how You can work on each one of us at the same time is beyond my ability to comprehend. Only You, God, can do this!

Only one with a true heart can truly lead and correct all other hearts. Your heart is to be trusted. Your words ring true.

In awe,
Laurie

Dear Laurel,

With all that said, remember to give Me all your cares. Give Me all that you are. You have no need to control anything. You cannot control how people think, or what they say, or how they react. You do not need approval from them. I see everything. I see your heart. I see your desire to represent Me well.

Grievous are the words of the accuser but I Myself AM working. I work as My Father has shown Me to work. I heal the heart. I surround you with true protection, and I see to every detail. You may not always perceive it, but I constantly work on your behalf.

Build up and edify your spiritual sisters and brothers in the most holy faith. They are worth every effort, and they shine like stars upon the earth. Listen carefully to My Spirit. Obey Him as He gives you words to speak, love to show, and life to impart. He will supply every good thing you need.

Seek Me first and be filled—for us and for our relationship. You will be able to minister out of the overflow, the excitement, and depth of our relationship. Let My revelation take root in you. Speak My Word.

Love,
Jesus

John 5:17 NASB

But He answered them, "My Father is working until now, and I Myself am working."

John 5:19 NASB

Therefore Jesus answered and was saying to them, Truly, truly, I say to you, the Son can do nothing of Himself, unless *it is* something He sees the Father doing; for whatever the Father does, these things the Son also does in like manner.

▶ **Where do you see Jesus at work in your life? How can you acknowledge that and thank Him?**

21

IAM

Dear Jesus,

love that You obey and display Your Father's will. You give me a free will to choose, but You also reveal Yourself and help me. Because of that, I can be who You've made me to be. I can do what You've called me to do. I need Your help so I don't shy away from that necessary process. I'm good at making myself so busy that *I don't get to it*. You already know that about me.

I'm grateful that Your Spirit always points me to You. The very interest and hunger I have for You comes from You. You have given me everything I would need for a life lived well with You.

Thank You for drawing me into prayer. Please hear my thoughts and prayers, and be gracious to answer. I do seek whole-heartedness! Is there someone who has wronged me that You want me to forgive and bless? Lead me as I examine my own heart.

May Your grace cover me, and may You keep me close. Grant me the power to resist sin. Thank You for the journey through this journal and through all the journals. Draw me back into them that I may obey what You have spoken.

I bless Your Name,
Laurie

Dear Laurie,

I AM continually revealing your own heart to you. I AM also continuously revealing Myself to you. The comparison shows you where you need to go, and where you need to improve. My Word is like a double-edged sword that cuts between the soul and the spirit. It is like a mirror that shows you your true self, and brings you into repentance.

How can you become whole if you are broken, yet think you are whole? When you see your need for a Savior, you welcome that Savior. When you think you are your own savior, you will be blinded to your real self. Deception and delusion are tricks and strategies of the enemy. That is why I'm calling you to a new level of prayer—that you would stay awake, be alert, and not be deceived.

I have good plans for you, but you must continually bring yourself into the truth of the Word and the Spirit. Deception and delusion can be very subtle. Many are those who fall for the tricks—often through pride and self-sufficiency. You are not your own savior.

Broken is the one who falls upon the Rock. I can restore such a one. I can even restore a repentant one who has been ground into powder. I can do all things because I AM.

Bow before Me and revere Me as your one and only Savior. I will continue to reveal Myself to you and I will be your Mediator so you will find the perfect will of God for your life.

Peace and grace to you,
Jesus

Mark 14:61-62 NASB

But He kept silent and did not answer. Again the high priest was questioning Him, and saying to Him, "Are You the Christ, the Son of the Blessed *One*?" And Jesus said, "I am; and you shall see THE SON OF MAN SITTING AT THE RIGHT HAND OF POWER, and COMING WITH THE CLOUDS OF HEAVEN."

John 8:58 AMPC

Jesus replied, I assure you, most solemnly I tell you, before Abraham was born, I AM.

Matthew 21:44 AMPC

And whoever falls on this Stone will be broken to pieces, but he on whom It falls will be crushed to powder [and It will winnow him, scattering him like dust].

Hebrews 4:12 NASB

For the word of God is living and active and sharper than any two-edged sword, and piercing as far as the division of soul and spirit, of both joints and marrow, and able to judge the thoughts and intentions of the heart.

▶ In what ways will you allow Jesus to reveal *Himself* to you? In what ways will you allow Jesus reveal *yourself* to you? What will you do to become more like Him?

22

Dear Jesus,

Thank You for hearing all the prayers for my well-being. Thank You for hearing the prayers for my family and for my church family. Thank You for keeping us in Your care, and for training us in Your ways.

Thank You for my beautiful family. Your grace and provision continue to astound me. Your presence surrounds me. Your kingdom fills me to overflowing.

Lord, as new challenges arise every day, strengthen and protect us. Rise up in us to meet every challenge with victory.

Yours,
Laurie

Dear Laurel-Crowned One,

I AM crowned with many crowns. I AM the Lord Your God! Nothing escapes My sight. Nothing passes through My hands without My perfect will and My complete approval.

I *have* and I *will* raise up a standard against the enemies that surround you, your family, and your church family. Many are overwhelmed by these enemies, but My standard is so bright and so awe-inspiring that every enemy's attack is stopped. They freeze in fear. I raise that standard for you.

I also raise the standard *in* you to become more like Me. I expect your thoughts and your words to become more loving, more gentle, and more affirming. Correct in love and encourage with grace—the grace that I have afforded you.

The distractions end now. Ask Me for the power to focus, and I will gladly give it to you. You have access to all things in Me. Every comfort, every grace, every tool, every weapon is Mine to give and yours to receive.

Begin an active campaign to bless with your mouth. I say it again—active campaign. Seek the opportunities, and you will find them. Power flows in love and grace. That power is to heal, to nurture, and to forgive.

I will extend your days. I will give you things to accomplish in My kingdom. The fields are ripe to harvest, and the workers are few. Some want position and power but I seek workers. It is time to work. It is time to pray, time to teach, and time to write. I will help you.

Keep your heart close to Mine. Keep your heart free from offense, fleshly desires, and petty jealousies. You are unique, you are uniquely called, you are uniquely anointed, and you are uniquely gifted. There should be no comparisons, no insecurities, and no wasted time.

Move when I say move, rest when I say rest. Wholeness is found in Me. Continue to ask Me and I will lead you by My Spirit.

Love,
Jesus

Exodus 16:12 NASB

"I have heard the grumblings of the sons of Israel; speak to them, saying, 'At twilight you shall eat meat, and in the morning you shall be filled with bread; and you shall know that I am the LORD your God.'"

Isaiah 41:13 NASB

"For I am the LORD your God, who upholds your right hand,
Who says to you, 'Do not fear, I will help you.'"

Isaiah 59:19 KJV

So shall they fear the name of the LORD from the west, and his glory from the rising of the sun. When the enemy shall come in like a flood, the Spirit of the LORD shall lift up a standard against him.

▶ **How can you come under the covering of the Lord your God in a greater way? How can you let Him lead you today and every day?**

23

I AM FAITHFUL

Dear Jesus,

Thank You for speaking to me by Your Spirit. You are faithful even when I am lax and unfaithful. You prompt me when I forget. You remind me when I've made a promise, and You reiterate Your Word when I need to hear the truth.

I always need You, even when I'm not aware. Sometimes I feel off-balance, and I'm not sure why. Sometimes I'm feeling frustrated, and I'm not sure why. Usually, it's because I have not spent enough time in Your Word or enough time listening to You.

Sometimes You and Your glory seem intangible to my mortal mind. I want to see You. I want to experience Your glory. Lord, help me get out of my mortal mind and into a spiritual mind. I know then that I will experience You and Your glory in a greater measure.

I am so blessed that I can pray in Your name and be answered. I am blessed to be Your child, God. I am indeed grateful.

Love,
Laurie

Dear Laurie,

Even when you are not faithful, I AM. My plans for My people are not dependent on your plans or your planning, but on Mine. Often, I cause things to work out whether you fully participate or not. I will use whoever follows Me and is willing—one whose heart is toward Me in humility and wonder.

I'm still working on you. I'm still polishing you. I'm still working on your motives. I'm showing you why you do the things you do. I'm showing you your identity. Listen to what I say concerning how I see you and what I want to do in you.

You saw and experienced a touch today concerning who you are and what I want you to do. You will do more of that (praying for healing and speaking My Word). I will cause others to trust My Spirit in you, and give you opportunities to speak My Word to them. Be careful to listen well, and check your heart often.

I AM also healing your body. I have heard your cries and have seen your days and years of suffering. I AM faithful to My word to restore you. I AM faithful.

Love,
Jesus

1 Corinthians 1:9 AMPC

God is faithful (reliable, trustworthy, and therefore ever true to His promise, and He can be depended on); by Him you were called into companionship *and* participation with His Son, Jesus Christ our Lord.

Revelation 19:11 AMPC

After that I saw heaven opened, and behold, a white horse [appeared]! The One Who was riding it is called Faithful (Trustworthy, Loyal, Incorruptible, Steady) and True, and He passes judgment and wages war in righteousness (holiness, justice, and uprightness).

▶ **He is faithful even when we don't yet see the results. How can you rest in His faithfulness today?**

24

Dear Jesus,

press in today. I need You. Forgive me for chasing weak activity and for not seeking You first. Again, I have gotten ahead of myself and ahead of You. I still battle on a few different fronts.

Speak over me, Lord. Speak Your freedom and life into me. Cause the kingdom of God to be displayed in me. Set me free from every form of opposition that would get in the way of You working in me. I ask You to fight for me. When You fight, You win. You always achieve victory.

I give You thanks for who You are, what You do, and what You are going to do. You are my King and I pray You take control of every situation. I love Your loving-kindness. I will be reminded to trust You, Lord.

Love,
Laurie

Dear Laurie,

Thoroughly, I have loved you. Your battle does not mean I love you less. In the midst of everything, I AM testing and refining your faith so you can shine for Me more and more.

Press in to My presence, and prove Me that My Word is true. I AM for you, and My Name will come forth through your victories.

I send to you My own divine healing. I paid for your sins and for your infirmities with My own suffering and life. I breathe life into you. Sense My presence and be peaceful. I AM the Prince of Peace dwelling in you. Fear and worry will not help you. Allow My peace to fill you and to help you. I'm right here!

Be careful what you say and how you say it. Doubt and unbelief from your mouth aid the cause of your enemies. Keep your heart and your mind set on Me. I will keep you in peace when you do. Rest in Me.

Love,
Jesus

Isaiah 9:6 AMPC

For to us a Child is born, to us a Son is given; and the government shall be upon His shoulder, and His name shall be called Wonderful Counselor, Mighty God, Everlasting Father [of Eternity], Prince of Peace.

Isaiah 26:3 NKJV

You will keep *him* in perfect peace, w*hose* mind *is* stayed *on You,* because he trusts in You.

John 14:27 NASB

Peace I leave with you; My peace I give to you; not as the world gives do I give to you. Do not let your heart be troubled, nor let it be fearful.

► **How can you let the Prince of Peace Himself rule your heart and mind today?**

25

Dear Jesus,

I have asked You to be near, and You are. You are right here. Your promises are sure and true. Your voice is clear, and Your faithfulness is evident in my life. Just when I think things are not going to work out, they do. Just when I think things will not change or get better, they do. I know it's You at work on my behalf. Thank You, Lord.

Thank You for the opportunity to rest, to invite Your presence, and to be restored. Holy Spirit, You are welcome anytime. Teach me and help me. Show me the truth as only You can.

Lord, fill me with Your joy. Help me to live in the present and enjoy Your blessed company.

Love,
Laurie

Dear Laurel,

In all that seems to be failure, you have victory in Me. In all that seems to be difficult, you have victory in Me. In all that seems to be weak, you have victory in Me. Lean on Me. Continually ask Me for My presence, My victory, and My miracles. I AM with you always.

Life experience and My Spirit cause you to see things in yourself. I'm putting My finger on and cleaning up your motives. Your heart and your thoughts have been fearful, and I will help you think more securely.

I AM mighty, and I never lose. I surround you like a shield as I fight for you. Out of My mouth come words of victory, creative power, and weaponry that no one can imagine. I love and defend My Creation and all that is Mine. I declare you to be Mine. No one else and nothing else can take you.

Be reminded of the details of that vivid dream I gave you long ago. I did not allow you to be overtaken. I protected you, nurtured you, and loved you as a dear one in Me. Nothing has changed. I have not changed, and I have not changed My mind about you.

I now bestow upon you a deep peace. As I AM peaceful, follow My lead. Let's walk together, so I can continue to show you My character and My ways. Cling to Me and trust Me for everything and in everything.

Love,
Jesus

Matthew 28:19-20 NKJV

Go therefore and make disciples of all the nations, baptizing them in the name of the Father and of the Son and of the Holy Spirit, teaching them to observe all things that I have commanded you; and lo, I am with you always, *even* to the end of the age. Amen.

Psalm 55:18 AMPC

He has redeemed my life in peace from the battle that was against me [so that none came near me], for they were many who strove with me.

▶ **Sometimes we think He is not with us. The Scriptures listed tell us that is not so. How can you reach out to Him today?**

26

Dear Jesus,

Thank You for Your favor. I thank You for the grace that rests upon my family and me amid difficulties. I am sometimes discouraged with the lack of progress in physical healing. I ask for Your divine healing. I ask You for miracles.

I thank You for reminding me to dance, play, and experience freedom in Your presence. I come before You as a child, helpless and needy. Thank You that You promise protection, light-heartedness and childlike freedom.

Also, thank You for bringing up my faults so they can be given to You and healed. You are the one and only God, and I worship You.

Love,
Laurie

Dear Laurel,

You walk with your crown tilted to one side as if your daughterhood is tainted because of sickness. It is only tilted if you believe I am not true to My word, that I am not necessarily good, or that you have not been good enough to receive My healing. None of this is true.

Your feelings and your circumstances have nothing to do with the fact that I AM good, I give unmerited favor, and I heal as part of My loving nature.

Straighten your crown, raise your head toward Me, and worship with joy. I tell you to be encouraged, speak with authority, and believe I AM good. I AM your healer, your strong tower, and your hiding place. I haven't forgotten you. I AM still working on you and in you. Your heart is sometimes yet divided and scattered. Keep pressing in. You're making good progress.

Love,
Jesus

Matthew 20:15 NKJV

Is it not lawful for me to do what I wish with my own things? Or is your eye evil because I am good?

Acts 10:38 AMPC

How God anointed *and* consecrated Jesus of Nazareth with the [Holy] Spirit and with strength *and* ability *and* power; how He went about doing good and, in particular, curing all who were harassed *and* oppressed by [the power of] the devil, for God was with Him.

Psalm 32:7 NKJV

You *are* my hiding place; You shall preserve me from trouble; You shall surround me with songs of deliverance. *Selah.*

▶ **Let the truth that God is good permeate your thoughts today. In what ways can you meditate on His goodness?**

27

Dear Jesus,

I am grateful for You. I don't know where I would be without You. I cringe to think of what I would be like and what I would be doing. Thank You for being the truth in my life and for progressively rescuing me from myself.

I ask for Your wisdom and peace as I walk through this life. Lord, let Your power rise up in me. I need the power of Your Spirit to think well, to feel well, to speak well, and to act well. You did warn us that it wouldn't be easy. The best thing is when I realize I can't do life without You. I need You every step of the way.

I love to study Your Word. I find something new every time! Even if I've read a particular passage or story many times, You always show me something wonderfully new. I'm so excited that Your Word never gets boring. In it are layers of insight and wisdom that I can't wait to uncover. Lord, draw me in.

Love,
Laurie

Dear Laurel,

I AM the Word and My Word is all-powerful. It will remain so for all eternity. In it is life, and the best life for you. In it are the secrets of the kingdom of God. In it are words, tools, and insight you need to keep your eyes on things above and not below. Do not let your heart be troubled. I AM aware of everything that happens, and I AM in charge.

I AM faithful to My promises. I AM faithful to My people. I will cause My good plans to unfold in all your lives. Be careful to watch and to listen. My Spirit will teach you in the Word, and in the way you should go.

Remain in My presence. I am getting ready to reveal more of My divine character to you. My presence will do a healing and cleansing work in My people. Lives will be changed. Hearts will be mended and filled to overflowing with Me. Ears will be opened and tongues will be loosed. Heat, glory, and overwhelming power will come forth from My presence. Look for Me. Thank you for expecting Me with anticipation. I'll be there.

Love,
Jesus

John 1:1 NASB

In the beginning was the Word, and the Word was with God, and the Word was God.

Matthew 24:35 NKJV

Heaven and earth will pass away, but My words will by no means pass away.

► How can you meditate on the Word today? How can you use the Word to right a wrong, to declare divine assistance, or to worship Him?

28

Dear Jesus,

Thank You for doing so many wonderful things in Your church. You are truly with us. Continue to guide us as we minister to others. Fill us with more of Your Spirit so we can minister well—according to Your ways and not our own ways. I don't want to get ahead of You, and I don't want to lag behind You. More than anything, I want to accurately represent You in every way.

Lord, I am grateful for You, for Your ongoing friendship, and for Your communication. You are my biggest blessing. I am also grateful for Your perfect heart and for Your perfect motives. You never seek to harm me, but You seek to make me holy and whole. Thank You for giving me a season of health and well-being. What a difference! I forgot what it felt like to be well. I'm blessed to experience it again.

Guide me, I ask, in the days and weeks coming, that I may hear and obey Your Spirit. May I move as You say to move.

Love,
Laurie

Dear Laurie,

Holiness is part of My Name. I constantly seek those whose hearts are pure toward Me. All of heaven cries, 'Holy, holy, holy is the Lord God Almighty.' Heaven has touched earth when people join in this praise.

Brokenness before Me happened yesterday during church services. Hearts were humbled, cleansed, healed, and refreshed. You allowed and made room for the Holy Spirit to do His good work. He is busy on the earth, and He is working in the hearts of My people. Many respond to Me, but they don't always realize it's Me leading them. Someday, they will discover it was Me all along.

I AM drawing hearts from every nation, every tribe, and every tongue. My will shall be accomplished on the earth. I will build My church.

Hope is powerful. When My people have hope, they can go on and follow My leading. When hope is broken, their hearts fail and faint. I AM your living hope. I live on the inside of you. I cause you to hope—to hope in My goodness, My plans, and My love for you. Express these things to others. Some are losing hope in humanity. They are looking for hope in the wrong places. Direct them toward Me. Remind them the power to hope comes from living hope dwelling inside them— Me. I will guide them and lead them home.

Love,
Jesus

1 Peter 1:3-5 NASB

Blessed be the God and Father of our Lord Jesus Christ, who according to His great mercy has caused us to be born again to a living hope through the resurrection of Jesus Christ from the dead, to *obtain* an inheritance *which is* imperishable and undefiled and will not fade away, reserved in heaven for you, who are protected by the power of God through faith for a salvation ready to be revealed in the last time.

1 Timothy 1:1-2 NASB

Paul, an apostle of Christ Jesus according to the commandment of God our Savior, and of Christ Jesus, *who is* our hope, to Timothy, *my* true child in *the* faith: Grace, mercy *and* peace from God the Father and Christ Jesus our Lord.

► **What makes you discouraged or hopeless? How does your perspective change in light of Jesus, the living hope inside of you?**

29

I AM ABLE

Dear Jesus,

I honor You. I give You credit for every good thing, for every positive outcome, and for every victory. I love it when I ask for help, and You help me. I don't ever want to take that for granted, or to think I fixed everything myself. I get that You're the only one who can truly work things out well.

I have consciously worked on agreeing with Your Word and not speaking negatively or hopelessly about issues. I have not experienced complete success in this realm, but I'm making progress. I see the difference it makes when I agree with You—in my heart and out loud. I hate to think of how many times I have derailed myself in my life by not agreeing with what You say. Your Word says much about You, and it says much about life itself.

Lord, I ask You to speak. Help me to recognize, to absorb, and to understand all You say to me. Help me to be who You say I can be. Help me to rejoice in the present, and to look forward with great hope. I welcome You.

Love,
Laurie

Dear Laurie,

Time is of the essence. Gather within yourself the urgency to love and to assist the ones who are confused, aimless, or filled with doubt. Things have happened to them, and they may welcome the help if asked.

I AM able to instruct, to lead, and to strengthen. I AM able to untangle the thoughts and the feelings on the inside. I AM able to give courage to say and to do the right things. I can steady those who need stability. I can comfort those who mourn, and heal those who are wounded.

Holiness is My goal—holiness in My people. I hover over their chaos and mourn over their losses and their choices. I love to restore and bring wholeness to My Creation. That's why I came—to restore what has been stolen or lost.

Be an open door for the good news of the Gospel. Speak with love, care, and consistency. Be a constant teacher of the Word and a conduit for Me. Speak what I tell you to say to each one. Provide the food of the Word, and display the fruit of the Spirit. Let your gifts flow. Be My witness upon the earth.

Love,
Jesus

Matthew 9:27-29 NASB

As Jesus went on from there, two blind men followed Him, crying out, "Have mercy on us, Son of David!" When He entered the house, the blind men came up to Him, and Jesus *said to them, "Do you believe that I am able to do this?" They *said to Him, "Yes, Lord." Then He touched their eyes, saying, "It shall be done to you according to your faith."

▶ God is able to do anything according to His good will. What can you entrust to Him today as the God who is able?

30

I AM TRUSTWORTHY

Dear Jesus,

Thank You, Lord, for hearing my prayers as well as the prayers of others on my behalf. I deeply appreciate the peace You bring to my heart. You're the only one who can.

I'm still amazed, however, at how quickly I can become unnerved by a new kind of issue or a seemingly insurmountable one. You would think I would know by now to run to You before I try to figure everything out myself. Oh Lord, help. Forgive me for worrying or doubting. You always do come through—not always in the way I expect, but in Your best way.

As I go through trials with You, I learn better how to have more grace and compassion on others. I realize they are also in the midst of their life's trials. Compassion is so powerful, and I'm grateful for the lessons. I know I pray differently because of these lessons. I know I love more because of these lessons. I know You are growing my character. I know You know what You're doing.

The good news is that I come around quicker each time. I remember how You've helped me before, and I set my expectation that You will help me again. I want to get to the place where no matter what, I am always peaceful and trusting.

Love,
Laurie

Dear Laurie,

Holy is My Name, and holy is My countenance. I constantly speak My Name over you, and I shine My countenance on you. You still have some fear and doubt, but you are one who has a pure heart toward Me. You look for Me with expectation. You are aware of the temporal nature of the world's systems. They can't help you to the degree I can, and you know that.

My heart is compassionate toward all who suffer and are oppressed. You say you want to be like Me, so this is an area I will continue to make known to you. Your heart is becoming more like Mine. You have asked, and I have answered.

Keep your eyes fixed on Me. Pray constantly, and trust Me. Work with Me on everything instead of trying to fix everything yourself. Lean on Me fully. Bring your petitions before Me early. Lay your heart out before Me, and do not restrain yourself. I AM trustworthy. You will not be disappointed.

Love,
Jesus

1 Corinthians 1:9 AMPC

God is faithful (reliable, trustworthy, and therefore ever true to His promise, and He can be depended on); by Him you were called into companionship *and* participation with His Son, Jesus Christ our Lord.

Revelation 1:5-6 AMPC

And from Jesus Christ the faithful *and* trustworthy Witness, the Firstborn of the dead [first to be brought back to life] and the Prince (Ruler) of the kings of the earth. To Him Who ever loves us and has once [for all] loosed *and* freed us from our sins by His own blood, and formed us into a kingdom (a royal race), priests to His God and Father—to Him be the glory and the power *and* the majesty and the dominion throughout the ages *and* forever and ever. Amen (so be it).

▶ We serve a trustworthy God. What do you need to trust Him with today?

31

I AM ALIVE FOREVERMORE

Dear Jesus,

Thank You for feeding me in Your Word today. In allowing myself to fear, I have caused my own trouble. I embrace Your encouragement, endurance, steadfastness, patience, wisdom, and faith. As I'm getting things done today, I'm trusting You to make up for what I lack.

Help me to keep my eyes on You and Your goodness. I thank You that You are forever, and that You rule all Creation. How beautiful and wonderful of You to create us as eternal beings to have relationship with You forever!

Lord, You see what I experience in life, and how sometimes I get discouraged. Lord, I ask You to encourage me—give me courage! Remind me that I do have Your favor. Your comfort is true comfort for the soul and the spirit. Thank You for having patience with me.

Love,
Laurie

Dear Laurie,

There is often struggle to win the prize, to win the race, and to wear the crown. Endurance, steadfastness, and patience are fruit of the struggle toward My ways. They come out as fruit of My Spirit and display Me, especially in trying or difficult circumstances. I AM doing a work in you. Don't you think I know what's happening? I create personal tests for you so you will learn, grow, and pass. You will get there. Your demeanor has improved. Your fear eases off as you read My Word. You gain courage as you listen to My Spirit, and as you are reminded of My sovereignty, love, and character. You are better when you remember who I AM.

I know you have been sad, and I know you are eager to hear about your beloved sister who continually lives in My presence. She makes offerings of gold to Me. I AM her King, her benevolent protector, the one who rescued her, and the one who loves her as My own, precious creation. Those who are humble and wise bring Me gold. It is the best of who they are, and they give it as an offering.

There is a winsome grace about her worship—that of a grateful heart. She is aware of the suffering and torment that exists apart from Me. Her soul feels and realizes the safety and surrounding of My presence.

She sees and loves you all from a pure heart that fears no more. She belongs to a great cloud of witnesses that cheers on, prays for, and encourages you all. She pays great attention to her son, his wife, and their children. Her love for them abounds. She does not experience that dire "missing" of them that she thought she would. Time and space are different in the heavenly realm, and her joy has increased.

I tell you and assure you she is well, and it is well with her soul. You will see her again someday, and there will be much joy. Rest in this understanding and trust that I AM alive forevermore!

Love,
Master

Revelation 1:17-18 NKJV

And when I saw Him, I fell at His feet as dead. But He laid His right hand on me, saying to me, "Do not be afraid; I am the First and the Last. I *am* He who lives, and was dead, and behold, I am alive forevermore. Amen. And I have the keys of Hades and of Death."

▶ **Our living Jesus knows all things, and comforts us with all He is. How do these words bring comfort to you today?**

32

I AM MEEK AND HUMBLE

Dear Jesus,

Thank You for strengthening me so I can help others. I praise You for giving me life and well-being. Your faithfulness is real, and Your power is unlimited. I am constantly refreshed by Your presence.

I worship You for who You are. I am constantly in awe concerning how You know my heart. You always know exactly what I need and when I need it. The timely coincidences that happen in my life are more likely Your divine appointments. You bless me, and I love to bless others. You never waste an opportunity!

I'm most impressed with the fact that You could have come to this world with an imposing, overpowering demeanor toward all. Instead, You came with a humble manner and kind ways. Your example helps me lead better, knowing it's how You would want me to lead.

Lord, send Your Spirit continually, and stir Him up in me that You would be formed in me. Flood me with Your goodness, and help me develop Your character in my life.

Love,
Laurie

Dear Laurie,

Continue to come into My presence and rejoice! I encourage you to allow yourself times of rejoicing. Look for things to be joyful about! If you look, you will surely find them.

The ones you promise to pray for—write a new list and put it in the cover of your journal. Spend time praying for them. Many need prayers, and I will lead you in prayer by My Spirit.

Praise My Name and worship Me at every opportunity. Your perspective will change. This is a journey of faith and of adventure. It is an Opportunity for Me to prove Myself in your life and in the lives of others. Make My Name great upon the earth!

I say to you, 'Diligence, diligence, diligence.' Keep seeking Me, and keep learning. There is always much to learn. Learn of Me for I AM meek and humble. Yoke yourself to Me. I will show you. Come!

Love,
Jesus

Matthew 11:29 AMPC

Take My yoke upon you and learn of Me, for I AM gentle (meek) and humble (lowly) in heart, and you will find rest (relief and ease and refreshment and recreation and blessed quiet) for your souls.

▶ **How can we show meekness and humility today as we serve God and others? How can we grow in this aspect of Christlikeness?**

33

Dear Jesus,

May Your Name continually be made great upon the earth. I ask for Your Spirit to give me the breath and life to speak what You want me to speak with grace, truth, and boldness.

Lord, I pray for the atmosphere to continue to shift toward Your ways and Your kingdom. Kingdom of God, flood every heart and every mind. Lord, lead us by Your Spirit. Help us stay on course with our spiritual eyes and ears open to You. Lead the way, and help us make progress in character, morality, kindness, and love.

Thank You for helping me teach and preach according to Your will. I open my mouth, and I trust You to fill it. Let every word hit its mark for the glory of Your Name.

Love,
Laurie

Dear Laurie,

I will, I will, I will fill your mouth with breath and with words from Me. This is a crucial time in the world and in the kingdom. People need to know the plan—the plan of salvation, of maturity, and of a church that *must* rise above every attack, every enemy, and the temptations of the flesh.

I will build My church. I AM the Alpha and the Omega, the Beginning and the End. I know and execute the plans of each season in its time. The season is about to turn, and My church is a large part of it. You must rise up as a church and be who I have made you to be—not a self-centered arm, not a political arm, not a prideful arm, but the extension of My arm on the earth.

The church must go about led by the Spirit, doing good, preaching the Gospel in love and humility. Personal agendas are over. There will no longer be room for those who wrangle for position or for accolades. My anointing will draw those who need Me. Human structure for structure's sake will not stand, but the structure of the kingdom that flows in Me will be flexible and strong. It will withstand every false accusation. It will survive and overwhelm the mockers and the naysayers.

I have overcome all, and I have put the Spirit of the Overcomer inside you. Overcome lies with truth. Overcome hatred with love, and overcome your own flesh by the power of the Holy Spirit.

Love,
Jesus

Revelation 22:13 NASB

I am the Alpha and the Omega, the first and the last, the beginning and the end.

John 16:33 NASB

These things I have spoken to you, so that in Me you may have peace. In the world you have tribulation but take courage; I have overcome the world.

▶ **How can we remember today that He has a plan for every season, and He knows the beginning and the end of all things?**

34

I AM THE VINE

Dear Jesus,

Lord God, You are sovereign over all, and You are sovereign over me. I ask You to show me the way You have planned for me. In the past, Your words and impressions gave me something at which to aim. What a motivator! Without that, I would have floundered badly. Forgive me for any indifference and for the occasions when I neglect to follow the vision You have shown to me.

My place is in You. Cause calm order and creativity to take over. I wholeheartedly welcome that. Your Word reminds me who You are. When I'm reminded of who You are, I am reminded of who I am. You give me an identity that grounds me. The kind of identity You give is one that lasts! In that identity, I know I can do what You have shown to me.

In the midst of moving along with You, I praise You for causing discomfort to ease off in my body. Thank You for hearing prayers and for providing medicine that helps as You heal.

Love,
Laurie

Dear Laurie,

Limitations need not be limiting. You have access to all you need in Me. I will feed My strength to you. I will give ability to you. My wisdom will fill you. My hand will sustain you. My breath will breathe life into you.

Stay united with Me as a branch is attached to the vine. Truly I tell you, I AM the Vine and you are a branch. You must remain in Me to stay strong. You can only bear fruit to the degree that you are well attached to Me.

Listen closely as I instruct you concerning where you are to focus your efforts and to spend your time. Do spend more time doing wellness activities. You have not been balanced in that respect. Do write every day. Do pray often and listen well. You will sense My leading by listening to Me, and you will find much of My leading as you work. The needs and opportunities will be presented to you, and you will sense My leading. As you stay connected to Me, you will see it all unfold.

Love,
Jesus

John 15:1-5 NASB

I am the true vine, and My Father is the vinedresser. Every branch in Me that does not bear fruit, He takes away; and every *branch* that bears fruit, He prunes it so that it may bear more fruit. You are already clean because of the word which I have spoken to you. Abide in Me, and I in you. As the branch cannot bear fruit of itself unless it abides in the vine, so neither *can* you unless you abide in Me. I am the vine, you are the branches; he who abides in Me and I in him, he bears much fruit, for apart from Me you can do nothing.

▶ Is there something in your life that seems fruitless? If so, what area of your life needs better connection with the true Vine?

35

Dear Jesus,

I am so glad that I have You to admire, to follow, and to emulate. Your words have ultimate power, and yet You're gracious and humble. You never say too much. You speak kindly and directly as you correct me and encourage me. I guess that's You showing me how to communicate well with others.

Lord, have mercy on me for the times I operate in pride or fear. I know these are rooted in insecurity. We both know that works against working well with others. Lord! I ask You to stir up the Holy Spirit in me! Thank You for the gift of Your Spirit to teach me and to convict me. My desire is that I would have so much of You that my demeanor would truly resemble Yours.

Blessed be Your merciful Self, and blessed be Your holy Name.

Love,
Laurie

Dear Laurie,

You have My grace and My mercy. Continue to let My Spirit expose things, even seemingly small things within you that are harmful. Follow My lead, and be peaceful. Trust My Father in all things. If you do as I do and be at peace, issues will resolve without you fretting or trying to get your way. You'll experience My way, which is infinitely better.

These issues *are* all rooted in an insecurity that makes you think you will not get what you need. I AM the Bread of Life! You need nothing more. Feed yourself on Me and on My Word! You will gain strength and life on the inside. It will overflow in every area of your life.

Your path and others' paths are supposed to interact in a better way than they do. You all need more grace, more forgiveness, more collaboration, and more teamwork. We all do things better together. That's how the kingdom works. Stay close to Me. I'll continue to show you the way. You're learning and you're doing well.

Love,
Jesus

John 6:35 AMPC

Jesus replied, I am the Bread of Life. He who comes to Me will never be hungry, and he who believes in *and* cleaves to *and* trusts in *and* relies on Me will never thirst any more (at any time).

John 6:51 NASB

I am the living bread that came down out of heaven; if anyone eats of this bread, he will live forever; and the bread also which I will give for the life of the world is My flesh.

▶ **Are you feeling weak in any area of life? Feed on the Bread of Life today. Be filled with His goodness and His strength!**

36

Dear Jesus,

You are my only constant. Your love is always present. Your wisdom is endless. Your holiness is complete. Your understanding is perfect.

Lord, I want to seek Your face more than I seek Your hand. Remind me to love You for You. My heart is heavy, and I may know why. You seek my attention, and all I do is work. My Sabbath rest is still out of order, and in that, my part of our relationship fails.

Lord, draw me by Your voice. Sing over me. Cause me to hear You. Let my mind be focused on You and Your beautiful Self.

I choose rest, and I choose relationship today.

Love,
Laurie

Dear Laurie,

The distractions around you, including the media devices, are purposely addictive and draw you in to waste your time. I'm right here. I can be found.

Spend time worshiping. Spend time talking to Me—not asking for things, just talking. Even in your resting times, keep your thoughts on Me.

Don't worry about what the earthly "powers that be" think of you. You've already earned a reputation as a hard worker. Continue to work on your anointing, which is Me. In all your work, in all your words, in your heart, and in your attitude, display Me, the Anointed One. I AM He.

You've described people with anointing as ones who have spent time with Me in prayer. Be one of those people. You have the opportunity. You have the ability in Me. You have the capacity. You have to make room for Me. Very few are willing and able to empty "other things" out of their lives, especially in wealthy societies.

Empty yourself of your own pride—the flesh that desires to be propped up or inflated. This includes your personal aspirations and your desire for approval. Because you're in Me, the world will not approve of you, but I will. Seek My approval, not theirs.

I see how you are often viewed as 'less than' because of your gender. The anointing will continue to put that to rest in many cases. You can't push your way in the kingdom. Do it My way, and I'll take care of what you need.

Read this again. Often.

Love,
Jesus

John 13:19 NASB

From now on I am telling you before *it* comes to pass, so that when it does occur, you may believe that I am *He.*

John 18:4-6 NASB

So Jesus, knowing all the things that were coming upon Him, went forth and *said to them, "Whom do you seek?" They answered Him, "Jesus the Nazarene." He *said to them, "I am *He.*" And Judas also, who was betraying Him, was standing with them. So when He said to them, "I am *He,*" they drew back and fell to the ground.

▶ Jesus—He is the Anointed One. How can you live in His anointing in a greater way today?

37

Dear Jesus,

It's good to be in Your presence! In these times, You strengthen me and heal my soul. You speak life over me in Your Word. I rejoice as I sense *You* rejoice in these times of fellowship. You continually teach me how to *be*.

I am grateful that You work out the challenges of the day as well as the challenges of the week. Thank You for Your continuing strength and healing virtue. Thank You for Your comfort, Your favor, Your provision, and Your blessing.

I ask for wisdom for life's every thought and life's every move. In that Lord, I know that one small issue in my day can attempt to steal my joy. May Your wisdom and joy cause me to step over any and every issue, and to move on with my day. Please guide me, cover me, and lead me. Lord Jesus, lead the way. I choose You.

Love,
Laurie

Dear Laurie,

Long may you live to proclaim My goodness. May you be fruitful in the kingdom and lead many to the love of God, the Word of God, and the grace of God. You will continue to need and require more of My presence. You can do nothing without Me. Your time in My presence will fill you so you can overcome any and all difficulties.

Steadiness and faithfulness display My kingdom, My character, and My Spirit. Do not be tempted to give up or to lose heart. Keep listening to the plans of the Lord God. Seek Me with all your heart and you will find Me. I AM a God who is near to you.

There is a church bell ringing in the Spirit calling many to come find Me. It is a bell of freedom, or liberty. The Spirit says, "Come." All who truly seek Me will find Me. Receive them in My love. To do that, you must be filled to overflowing with Me. Come.

Love,
Jesus

Jeremiah 23:23 NASB
"Am I a God who is near," declares the Lord, "And not a God far off?"

Acts 17:24-28 NASB
The God who made the world and all things in it, since He is Lord of heaven and earth, does not dwell in temples made with hands; nor is He served by human hands, as though He needed anything, since He Himself gives to all *people* life and breath and all things; and He made from one *man* every nation of mankind to live on all the face of the earth, having determined *their* appointed times and the boundaries of their habitation, that they would seek God, if perhaps they might grope for Him and find Him, though He is not far from each one of us; for in Him we live and move and exist, as even some of your own poets have said, 'For we also are His children.'

▶ I encourage you to embrace Him today. Feed on His Word. Worship Him. Spend time listening and journaling. He is very near to you.

38

Dear Jesus,

Sometimes believing seems easy, and sometimes it seems difficult. Sometimes I trust You for big things, and then I struggle to believe You for small things. What is that all about? Oh Lord, I want to believe You for everything! I'm grateful that You have given me faith, that You've called me into Your wonderful kingdom, and that You never leave me without help. You are a good and faithful God.

I ask for more consistency, and I realize much of that is my choice. As I choose to see things Your way and to trust You no matter what, the small things and the big things both get handled with faith. I know You want me to be stretched in my faith on a regular basis. I get it.

I praise You that You guide me into a deeper faith and into greater understanding. Help me to trust You even when I don't understand. In every case, You have been faithful. Please receive my grateful prayers of thanksgiving. You are always the best.

Love,
Laurie

Dear Laurie,

Not only have I given you a measure of faith, but I have given you examples in your generations to observe and to follow. Remember Paul speaking of Timothy along with his mother and grandmother? The same holds true today. You cannot fully understand the powerful example that faithful people pass down through their generations. Be sure to pass that faithfulness on to your generations!

I have seen you trust Me immediately on some issues, and then doubt in others. It is My intention to teach you to trust Me in all things. As you feed on My Word and continue to listen to Me, your faith will continue to grow. In that, your peace increases.

I cover you in every way. I carefully watch over you. I care about what happens to My own. I keep My promises about never leaving you nor forsaking you.

I AM the author and finisher of your faith. I give you faith, and I help you grow that faith. You have made progress, and you will make more as you seek Me for all things. Cling to Me. I hold you fast, and I tell you to hold Me fast. I will not let go. You are Mine.

Love,
Jesus

Hebrews 12:1-2 NKJV

Therefore we also, since we are surrounded by so great a cloud of witnesses, let us lay aside every weight, and the sin which so easily ensnares *us,* and let us run with endurance the race that is set before us, looking unto Jesus, the author and finisher of *our* faith, who for the joy that was set before Him endured the cross, despising the shame, and has sat down at the right hand of the throne of God.

▶ **How can you access His faith or stretch your faith today?**

39

I AM HOLY

Dear Jesus,

Your faithfulness and Your loving-kindness are sure, and they are real. You have brought my family through times and seasons, high points and low points, victories and tragedies. All the while, Your good presence remains.

Thank You for correcting me, polishing me, teaching me, and growing me in the fruit of the Spirit. Thank You for speaking to me in the quiet moments as well as in the public moments. Thank You for calling me, for allowing me to be fed, and for giving me the ability to feed Your people by example.

Lord, show me and lead me for this year. I ask You to reveal Yourself and Your plans. Grant me courage and fearlessness in the face of change.

Thank You for watching over us and for holding us close to You. I bow in reverence and thanksgiving to You, the perfect, living God.

Love,
Laurie

Dear Laurie,

I encourage you to continue these times of written communication with Me—often alone in the stillness with Me and often in groups. You will find progressive, specific revelation for your life, your choices, and for the steps to come in the church.

I AM holy and I call you to be holy. Filter your thoughts and your conversations. Be thoughtfully careful of every choice. Be ultra-careful with your own thoughts and attitudes. Your expression *must* reflect Me and the ways of the kingdom. Ask Me for help with this. You sometimes make that split-second decision to let out your own opinion. Allow the fruit of self-control to grow in you as you spread kindness and encouragement. You will bear more fruit in the process. Keep a can-do, wise, calm, problem-solving attitude. Others benefit from it and learn—not only from the process, but the from the prayerful, trusting attitude that is displayed through you.

Intimacy and identity are inexorably linked. (I had to look up the word inexorable; it's not a word I use. Merriam-Webster says that inexorable means: not to be persuaded, moved, or stopped; relentless). When one pursues Me in intimacy, identity is revealed, clarified, and put into focus. Lives are changed and put back on track. Often, the real issues in peoples' lives are based on broken identity and broken intimacy. Many bandages can be applied and will provide a temporary cover, but the underlying factors remain.

To move forward in the healing of the identity and intimacy issues, make every effort to provide venues, teaching, written materials, and time invested to allow Me to reveal and heal. "Church as usual" will not fix what ails the human soul. Some are not necessarily getting what they need, so they drift away. Many don't know what they need and try various substitutes.

Hope is a powerful thing. It puts vision and energy into motion that gains momentum. Spend time developing the vision I gave you, and mix it with excited hope. Listen together and encourage one another in Me. Allow My Holy Spirit free reign in you and among you. He is the driving force and the power in all you are and all you do.

Love,
Jesus

Leviticus 11:45 AMPC

For I am the Lord Who brought you up out of the land of Egypt to be your God; therefore, you shall be holy, for I am holy.

1 Peter 1:16 AMPC

For it is written, You shall be holy, for I am holy.

▶ **Honor Him and praise Him for His holiness! What areas of your life can reflect greater holiness?**

40

Dear Jesus,

As I read notes and letters from the past, I see great progress some areas of my journey with You, and a lack of progress in others. In some cases, I feel stuck and need clarity.

I know You're planning some real change in how we serve You, and how we "do" church. I realize our mindsets and perceptions need to change. I know it is important that changes begin with me. Speak to me about what those changes look like, and how my personal disciplines can be stronger in the Spirit. Already, I know one is that I need to study more of Your Word for my own growth.

I'm excited about what You may have in store for this coming season. Flood me with Your glory as I listen to Your voice. Please continue to have patience with me, and grant me the power of the Spirit that I need.

Love,
Laurie

Dear Laurie,

Remember to access Me and to walk with Me every step of the way. I will lead you. Check in with Me before you check in with your own soul. I AM your Source.

I encourage you to study Samuel the man from the Scriptures. Study his habits, his thoughts, his words, and his actions. He led in a tumultuous time, and he suffered. See how he kept connected to Me, and how he kept his habits that displayed his integrity. He anointed David as king and had to wait many years for the outflow of righteousness to manifest. He waited in hope to see the king restore corporate worship.

Hold onto Me in these days of change. Be excited for what I AM doing in you and in My church. Press into Me for what you need.

People can only follow what they know or what they see. Model relationship. Model grace. Model obedience. Allow My joy to fill you no matter what you are experiencing. Count it all joy. Show people the bigger picture of what I AM doing.

These attributes describe wholeness, which is My goal for individuals, leaders, families, and for the body of Christ.

Too much division in My body has been allowed through apathy, mismanagement of the mind and the heart—not to mention the flesh, the world system, and the enemy's attacks on individuals, leaders, families, and churches.

You must ask My Spirit to breathe on and to inspire My people. You must ask Me to put a hunger in My people. You must pray for these specific things. You must teach these lessons in word and in deed. I need My body to be awakened! I need My body to function! I need My body to be filled and whole. I need My body to move together in obedience.

I AM throwing a fishing net over the earth. I AM casting My nets and I will bring in a big catch. I AM busy on the earth and I need you to join in. I can sovereignly do anything I choose, and I choose to do things in partnership with the body, My church, My people.

Know that you are chosen with love, with purpose, and with a plan. Nothing is out of control. No detail escapes My notice. Renew your mind in My Word. Listen. Obey. Let Me fill you, and watch Me work.

Love,
Jesus

1 Corinthians 8:5-6 AMPC
For although there may be so-called gods, whether in heaven or on earth, as indeed there are many of them, both of gods and of lords *and* masters, yet for us there is [only] one God, the Father, Who is the Source of all things and for Whom we [have life], and one Lord, Jesus Christ, through *and* by Whom are all things and through *and* by Whom we [ourselves exist].

Hebrews 5:9-10 AMPC
And, [His completed experience] making Him perfectly [equipped], He became the Author *and* Source of eternal salvation to all those who give heed *and* obey Him, being designated by God as High Priest according to the order of Melchizedek.

▶ God is your Source and is waiting for you to ask for what you need. Will you ask Him for yourself and for the body of Christ?

I pray you have grown closer to God as you have explored the great I AM. Be encouraged that He loves to hear from you, and He loves to speak to you.

As you continue to seek Him, you will continue to find treasures meant just for you! I encourage you to journal these treasures so you can revisit them and be reminded of His goodness.

Thank you for joining the journey. May you continue your journey, and may the Lord bless you continually!

Notes of Thanks

First, I thank God for who He is. He continues to keep us and lead us in the midst of all we encounter.

Second, I would like to thank by husband and children for their love and support. We are a good team!

Third, I thank Pastor Christopher Walker, a friend and colleague who models and teaches what it means to have a good relationship with God. He has taught me how to speak my heart, rest, and listen to the wonderful voice of God.

Last but not least, I thank each person who has decided to go on this journey to explore the love of God, the great I AM.

Printed in the United States
By Bookmasters